# I still Wanna be a.....

*Fantasies for Whatever Your Age May Be*

Surreal self-portraits and poetry
by Alisa Singer

Copyright © 2007 Alisa Singer
All rights reserved.

ISBN: 1-4196-8063-3

ISBN-13: 9781419680632

Visit www.booksurge.com to order additional copies.

## Note to Reader

During a recent visit to my son at school, I watched the students scurrying around campus headed for class, laughing and talking, laden with papers and books, and felt a surprising sensation. It was a form of envy — not so much of their youth (the perfectly toned bodies, shiny hair, smooth skin... okay, maybe a little) — but more of their energy, purpose and cheerful sense of confidence. They had all of their hopes before them, not yet "adjusted by reality". And I experienced a strong yearning to feel that way again. I wanted my dreams back — pure and untarnished. More precisely, it was not that I craved the innocent fantasies I nurtured as a twenty year old, but that I missed the optimistic spirit and soul that gave rise to them.

And so I set out to recapture that youthful state of mind. The whimsical self portraits and poetry in this book represent an exuberant exercise in denial of the limitations of age in the pursuit of our dreams. Taking on the surrealistic quality of a dream, they depict the realization by a middle-aged woman of long buried, but not quite forgotten, visions of childhood hopes and imagination. Unapologetically tacky, the images and poems remind us that, whatever our secret fantasies may be, age should never be an excuse. Clearly the form of our pursuits may change (half-century old bodies may not really sail gracefully across the stage and most of us have outgrown the desire to fly through the air ecstatically waving multi-colored pom poms). Though we may not retain the same aspirations we had when we were twenty, or even forty, we all must find (or perhaps rediscover) that thing we still yearn to be or to do, and about which we care deeply and earnestly, and then pursue it with a youthful sense of hopefulness and energy, a ready reserve of humor and a skin thickened by the wisdom of experience. Ultimately it matters little whether our aspirations are realized — by the mere act of holding fast to these passions we embrace a source of joy in our lives.

*(PS - In case the reader is wondering why there are no wrinkles or cellulite in these portraits of a fifty-something woman, please keep in mind these are, after all, my fantasies.)*

*Alisa Singer 2008*

"**Age** is a question of mind over matter. If you **don't** mind, it **doesn't** matter."

—SATCHEL PAIGE*

\* *Hall of Fame baseball player Satchel Paige was over 40 years old the entire time he played in the majors. He came out of retirement at the age of 60 to make a special appearance for the Kansas City Athletics and pitched 3 shutout innings.*

## DEDICATION

This book is dedicated to the loving memory of my most adored father Ralphie, who never let his age or health keep him from living and loving the delightful adventure of his life , and also to dear, precious Bubbie Fay, who always went where she needed to go and did what she needed to do and never paused for a moment to consider if it was appropriate for an 83 year-old grandmother to accept a job selling erotic lingerie.

# I still Wanna be a.....
## BALLERINA

I still wanna be a Prima ballerina,

Twirling 'cross the stage in my dainty tutu,

Balancing lightly on the tip of my sensible shoe.

                        But who will applaud my stunning debut?

                        Will I be praised in the morning review ?

                        More likely they'll say with no "ifs, ands or buts"-

                        "This lady's no dancer, She's merely a klutz!"

Then I'll exit the stage

With a neat pirouette,

And yell back at them –

**"You ain't seen nothin' yet!"**

# I still wanna be an... ASTRONAUT

I've packed all the stuff that I need to survive —
Mascara, oxygen, sunscreen (SPF Ten Thousand Five).
I'm ready for action, this is going to be fun,
My celestial adventures have finally begun.

Dazzling in my spacesuit of silver lame',
I'm the best looking chick in the Milky Way.
Reflecting the sun, you might call me a "hottie",
After all I am truly a heavenly body.

An idea comes to mind that leaves me quite cheery,
According to Einstein's space/time theory,
As long as I stay up here with these stars all a'twinkling,
I'll never grow older — that beats botox for wrinkling!

Suddenly I reverse throttle and head straight for home,
A nightmarish image has sent chills through my bones,
More frightening than being lost in space, forever alone,
Is the thought of the roaming charges on my cell phone.

Still, hurtling wildly through space is always good for some yuks,

I think I'll go back someday — after they open the first Starbucks.

# I still Wanna be a...
## BEAUTY QUEEN

I'M TALL AND STATUESQUE

IN MY EVENING GOWN,

I SHRIEK WITH DELIGHT

AS THEY PUT ON MY CROWN.

I WAVE AND BLOW KISSES,

MY CHEEKS ALL AGLOW.

AND WINK AT THE JUDGES,

AS THEY POCKET THEIR DOUGH.

# I still Wanna be a...

I wouldn't leap tall buildings in a single bound,
Catch people in mid-air, or chase criminals around.
And Lex Luthor wouldn't be my choice of adversary,
My foe would be someone much more ordinary.

I'd go after that villain we each keep inside our head,
That tells us to do this when we'd rather do that instead.
That tyrant of "supposed to", "ought to" and "should",
That commands us to keep pleasing and to always be good.

I'd destroy the evil forces that keep us from choosing,
Ways to spend time that we find most amusing.
Then released from the pressure of being painfully serious,
We'd experience the joy of being painlessly frivolous.

We'd put down our crossword puzzles, let our brain cells lie fallow,
And be free to embrace all things shamelessly shallow -

We'd be free to eat bread lacking in fiber,
And to become sugar-filled cola imbibers.
Free to scrap vegetables and go for fast food,
Or gobble down foie gras if we're in the mood.

Free to relax and find our own groove,
Or head for Las Vegas if we're bored with the Louvre.
Free to watch B-movies the critics will pan,
Free to admit you're a Barry Manilow fan.
Free to turn off the news and the history channel,
And turn on reality shows and American Idol.

Free to wear fishnet and dress in faux fur,
Or be hopelessly frumpy if that's what you prefer.
And if your thing is bling and lots of big hair,
I'd Wham! and Kazam! and then no one would care.

We'd be free to stop taking ourselves seriously
So we could write seriously bad poetry.
Free from gravity and free from pretense,
Free to indulge in absolute nonsense.
Free from the naysayers, and from the prudes,
Free to adopt a really bad attitude.

---

With my super powers I'd be the bold champion,
Of all things trivial, innocent and fun.
And if I succeed in my tasteless endeavor,
I'd be the most popular superhero ever.....

# I still Wanna be a...
## ROCKETTE

See me — look, there I am again!

All twelve feet are mine.

Each of my legs is 'bout four feet long,

In my fantasy chorus line.

        Each kick is perfectly synchronized.

        The audience is totally mesmerized,

        They're seeing a sight they will never forget,

        No one has ever yet cloned a Rockette!

*I still Wanna be a.....*

## GENIUS

It happened in a way I can't explain,
And I know it sounds a bit insane,
But today I grew a brand new brain,
Makes the old one seem like Shrimp Chow Mein.

I've grown a mustache and wild silver hair,
And another thing that's really weird,
I've figured out - "E=MC squared"!

People seek wisdom from my great mind,
"Please tell us if you're so inclined,
Which way is best for humankind?"

And I respond if I'm feeling talkative,
"My theory is — it's all relative."

# I still Wanna be a....
## CHEERLEADER

I sail through the clouds

On gigantic pom poms,

And when I land

I'm queen of the prom.


And of course I have

My pick of great dates.

No buff jocks for me,

Who's that guy…

something … Gates?

# I still Wanna be....
## TOO RICH &
## TOO THIN

They say "you can never be too rich or too thin",

But I know that's an unworthy goal.

Much better to strive for beauty of the mind,

And the reward of an unblemished soul.


Now I know skinny thighs and fat bank accounts

will not lead me to true happiness.

Still when I hear them say, "you never can be..."

Then the worst part of me, simply cries out with glee,

"Now there's a theory I think I'd like to test!"


And so slightly shamefaced, with a touch of chagrin,

I confess that I wanna be "too rich and too thin".

# I still Wanna be a.....
## BRAIN SURGEON

I look down at Bernie and feel a thrill,
And reach my hand out for the drill,
Palm extended, my commands are terse,
" Scalpel, forceps — suction nurse!"

Elbow deep in soft grey matter,
I work with care, try not to splatter.
At last I see it and exclaim "Aha!
I must rearrange Bernie's ganglia!"

        The crowd is watching me intensely,
        And I enjoy myself immensely,
        Promising that before I'm through,
        I'll save Bernie's life and double his IQ!

        Alas, alack, I'm just an attorney,
        Hard luck for my patient, dear old Bernie.
        Sadly, the companion of my medical journey,
        Lies cold and braindead on the gurney.

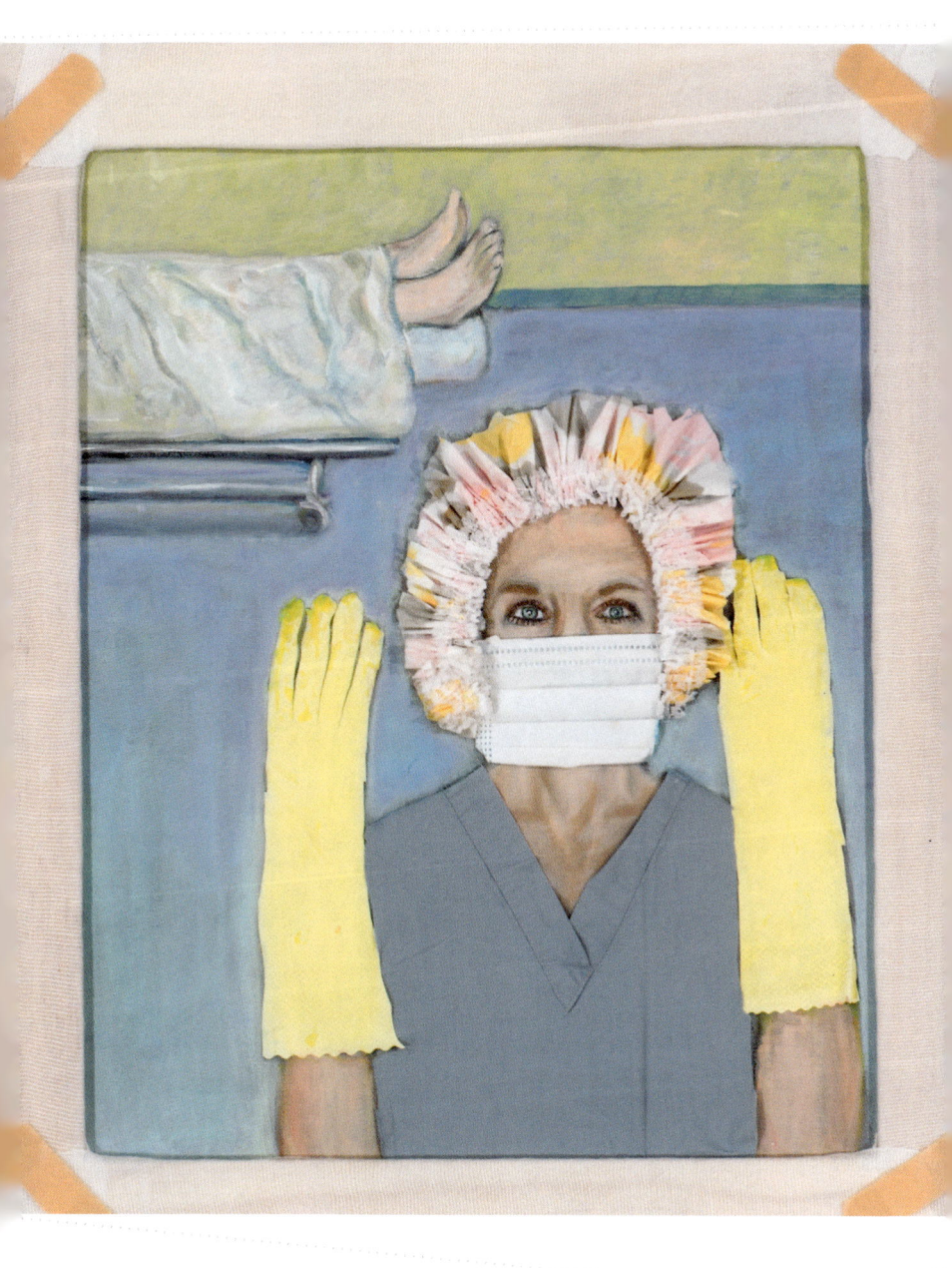

## I still Wanna be.....
# SERENE

I'm one with nature as you see,
No one is more one than me,
Try it and I'm sure you'll be,
No less than two, more likely three.


I've got my *Feng Shui* nailed down,
My *Yin* and *Yang* are quite renown,
I speak in three-part harmony,
And reek of healthy energy.


I'm tranquil when I meditate,
My mind achieves an altered state,
No wonder I'm so calm and gentle,
My "*Om*" is truly transcendental!


Gone is fear of bad hair days,
It's inner beauty my soul craves.
And I'd be feeling truly blessed,
If I could just uncross my legs!

# I still Wanna be..... BARBIE

You would think it would be easy,
Being 39"-21"-33".
But for a doll designed to glorify the feminine ideal,
I'm thinking she's gotten a pretty rotten deal.

For example, by the process of mathematical extrapolation,
We conclude she'd lack the body fat for regular menstruation.
Granted, there's the Scarlett O'Hara waist and that perky nose,
But she's condemned to stand in perpetuity on her tippy-toes.
She can never bend her knees or sit down for a spell,
And that hole in the bottom of her foot — oh cruel Mattel!

She may look pampered but this girl's got it tough.
No, it's definitely not Barbie I envy, I'm just after all her stuff.

I want the outfit that's just right for each and every occasion -
Barbie goes to prom, Barbie goes on vacation,
Barbie goes to the fraternity dance,
(What she does there is mere speculation.)

She's got the clothes to suit each exciting new career,
And like Madonna she recreates herself several times a year.
Barbie is a fashion editor, Barbie is an engineer,
Barbie is a glamorous supermarket cashier.
Barbie is a stewardess, Barbie is a nurse,
Barbie is a student teacher, Barbie drives a hearse.

Sure I want the dream house with the cool furniture,
But mostly I want her stunning wardrobe, each ensemble du jour,
Those elegant evening gowns with such style and allure,
The purses, hats and high-heeled shoes — the gloves so demure

The girl has fashion sense – she knows how to accessorize,
I crave each cunning detail of her varied merchandise.
But there is one accessory for which I clearly do not yen,
And that is for her dreary, dull stiff of a boyfriend — Ken.

# Further Reflections on Barbie

*(Why can't I stop?):*

Will we ever truly understand the
source of her fascination?

How does this doll capture and
enthrall each generation?

Perhaps part of the charm of this
captivating minx,

Is that she's about as approachable
as an Egyptian sphinx.

We know it's politically correct to
Critique her unreal physique,

And yet we can't deny the enduring
power of her mystique.

While we wrestle with our
ambivalence and continue
to obsess,

She remains serenely indifferent -
simply couldn't care less.

And she will triumph yet, for when
all is said and done,

Though she too approaches fifty,
there'll be no comparison.

We Boomers will watch our
"assets" sink and sag towards
our mid-section,

But Barbie's will remain infuriatingly
upright in eternal pert perfection.

*I still Wanna be....*

# PRESIDENT

My Fellow Americans -

It is with heartfelt appreciation,

And profound gratification,

That I accept my party's nomination,

With the hope to someday lead our nation.


And if you share my philosophy,

And my hopes for our great democracy,

Then please stand up and join with me,

And together we'll make history!

# I still Wanna be...ME

*(A Conversation With My Teenage Daughter)*

"Hey, what is all this wanna be stuff?" my daughter asks accusingly.
"You've always said 'accept yourself — that's the key to serenity'."
"Right you are!" I say with pride to my sweet, precocious offspring.
"But you can be who you are, and be glad to be you, and still
do anything."

"You don't need to be an opera star to sing a song.
Just open your mouth, take a breath, and sing along.
No need to be Ginger Rogers to get up and dance,
Just grab a partner, feel the beat, and take a chance.
And even if you don't become a celebrity gourmet,
No reason you can't learn to cook a really mean souffle'."

"You don't need to be an Olympic champion to go out and run,
You don't need a title or degree to do what you think is fun.
You don't…."

"Okay mom, I get your drift. I'll keep it all in mind.
And though I'm sure it's great advice, must you always speak in rhyme?
Wow — look at the time! Really gotta' go, though of course, I'd
love to stay,
Oh — one more thing I forgot to ask — who's Ginger Rogers anyway?"

# and you?

How about you?

Who do you wanna be?

What's your great
secret fantasy?

Would you be a rock star?

An astronaut?

A zillionaire cruising a hundred
foot yacht?

Sounds pretty silly?

Who cares diddly-squat!

Why not a nuclear physicist?

A famous Broadway lyricist?

A controversial Zionist?

A perky meteorologist?

Maybe you'll cure an
incurable disease,

Hang from one toe on
a circus trapeze.

Study the habits of aborigines.

Ski down a glacier or
conjugate Portugese.

All this you can do

And so very much more,

What you didn't do at twenty,

You must do at ninety-four.

So whether you're Clark Kent

Or Superman,...

Live out your fantasy

The best way you can.

Hang on to those dreams,

They're attached to your soul,

And never believe

You're too late or too old.

Kick up your heels

'fore you turn up your toes,

It's no big deal,

These days anything goes...

*Sail over the top, bold and rejuvenated*

*Aging with grace is just so overrated!*

When you wish upon a star,
　　　　makes no difference how old you are.

**MAY ALL YOUR DREAMS COME TRUE!!!**

Made in the USA